P9-APX-386

NEW YORK TRANSIT
MEMORIES

by Harold A. Smith

Quadrant Press, Inc.
Suite 707
19 West 44th Street
New York, NY 10036
☎ [212]-819-0822

In a photographic excursion such as this, we must begin with a big thank you to the many people who recorded and thereby preserved our memories of transit history. Their photographs have found their way into and become prized specimens for many collectors. This book contains a wide variety of photos that have been generously contributed or have been lent from valuable collections. These have been credited with great appreciation. Those photos that have come from my own collection are so noted and thus the only photos not credited were ones I myself have taken from time to time.

HAROLD A. SMITH
Ridgewood, NY
Summer, 1997

© **1997 by Quadrant Press, Inc.**

All rights reserved

ISBN 0-915276-56-9

CONTENTS

FRONT COVER:
The summer days of 1945 are pleasantly recalled by this dual-mode rail transit photograph. A train of BMT's unforgettable gate cars is seen crossing high above a then-modern PCC working its way down B&QT's Vanderbilt Avenue route in Brooklyn. —*Frank Reilly collection.*

INSIDE FRONT COVER:
One of the unheralded links between Manhattan and Queens was the Queensboro Bridge Railway, a streetcar operation running between an underground terminal loop at 60th Street & Second Avenue and the plaza in Queens. This often-overlooked line was New York City's last trolley operation. The line made a stop on the bridge to accommodate those wishing to go to Welfare Island, as Roosevelt Island was then called. The car in this scene was purchased from the Manhattan Bridge 3¢ Line.

TITLE PAGE:
The camera has caught three modes of transit at once near West Farms Square. Surface Transportation's GMC empty coach has edged Third Avenue Railways comfortably full car 667. Meanwhile, the IRT el speeds ahead unaffected by traffic. —*Bill Myers collection.*

ABOVE:
Rattan seats equip the interior of Staten Island Rapid Transit No. 308 in this May 15, 1960 view.

A BRIEF HISTORICAL REVIEW

The history of public transportation in New York City reaches back to the first part of the nineteenth century. It was the age of animal power, and in 1827 the first horse-drawn public coaches began operating up Broadway to Bleeker Street. Six years later, the New York & Harlem River Railroad used horses to pull the city's first railcars on the Bowery between Prince Street and 14th Street. This line reached Harlem in 1837. In 1884, the horse-drawn omnibuses on lower Broadway were replaced with horse-drawn railcars, and the use of horses declined rapidly as new technologies emerged. Nevertheless, horses would not be retired from the streets until 1917 when the last horse-car route made its final run on Bleeker Street.

One of the first new technologies was the cable car. In 1886, a cable car line was opened on 125th Street. An extensive cable car system was envisioned, but expansion ended as quickly as it began when the first electric streetcar line was opened on Jamaica Avenue in Queens County the following year. It extended to East New York in Brooklyn.

The superiority of electric propulsion was so unquestionable that almost all of Brooklyn's horsecar lines were converted to electric operation between 1891 and 1895. Manhattan lines were also electrified, but because of the proliferation of power, telegraph, and telephone lines above the street, the city mandated the use of underground facilities. In order for streetcars to comply, a "conduit" system was employed. Instead of an overhead wire, this method used a third rail located beneath the street to supply power. The power rail was reached through a slot between the rails by a "plow" under the streetcar. Cable lines, already having a slot for access to the cable, were a natural for conversion.

Just as horsecars were converted to electric operation, the Fifth Avenue Coach Lines converted its horse-drawn omnibus line using the city's first gasoline-powered motor buses. The service that had begun on July 25, 1896 between Bleeker Street and 89th Street had open-top double-deckers running between Washington Square and 90th Street starting July 1, 1907. Closed-top double-deckers did not enter service until the chill of February 2, 1922. The open-top double-deckers made their last runs December 28, 1946 and the closed-top ones, April 27, 1953. A brief comeback was attempted in the 1970s when new double-deckers from British Leyland arrived. A failure, they later wound up running in San Francisco.

The first elevated railway was the Greenwich Street and Ninth Avenue line in Manhattan, a single-track cable-operated line opened in 1870. Running between Dey Street and 29th Street with no intermediate stops, its operations were not successful until 1871 when the

line was converted to steam power and extended to connect South Ferry with 59th Street. By 1889, there were elevated lines on Ninth, Sixth, Third, and Second Avenues, and in Brooklyn on Myrtle, Lexington, Fifth Avenues, Fulton Street and Broadway. By 1902, the steam-powered Third Avenue el had reached Bronx Park. The first multiple-unit electric el train tested successfully on the Second Avenue el in 1900, and in the next three years, the Second & Ninth Avenue lines were electrified.

New York's first subway was a demonstration model built by the Beach Pneumatic Transit Company and opened under Broadway in Manhattan from Murray Street to Warren Street in 1868. It consisted of a single compressed-air-propelled 22-passenger car operating in a 312-foot long, 9-foot-diameter tube. Over 400,000 people paid 25\242 each to ride it, but this curiosity failed to attract investors.

The city's first electrically-operated subway was opened in 1904 by the Interboro Rapid Transit. It ran from City Hall via what are now the Lexington Avenue, Grand Central Shuttle, 7th Avenue, 145th Street & Lenox Avenue lines, the new subway was equipped with the first all-steel subway cars bought from the Gibbs Company. Similar equipment was bought by the Long Island Rail Road. In 1910, the LIRR was acquired by the Pennsylvania Railroad and operated into the then brand-new Pennsylvania Station. After 1910, new LIRR electric cars used the PRR's own body design and, in 1927, the LIRR became the first railroad to have completely replaced all wooden passenger cars with steel ones.

In 1910, the Hudson & Manhattan Railroad Company opened the first underwater rapid transit tunnel. It had planned extensions to Astor Place and to Grand Central and actually built a tunnel under Sixth Avenue as far as 42nd Street. Although it never ran beyond 33rd Street, the unused tunnel from 35th Street to 40th Street ultimately became a pedestrian tunnel above the IND Sixth Avenue subway, tiled to match the IND stations. Due to uncontrolled crime, it was sealed at both ends in 1993 with walls made to match the IND station mezzanines.

William McAdoo, president of the Hudson & Manhattan, sought to compete with the giant Interboro Rapid Transit and submitted a plan to the Public Service Commission for three subway extensions to the H&M. Potential investors were reluctant to oppose the powerful Interboro. Ultimately, the H&M went bankrupt and in 1964 the Port Authority of NY and NJ bought it and reorganized it as the Port Authority Trans-Hudson (PATH).

Only the powerful Brooklyn Rapid Transit challenged the IRT by extending its routes into Manhattan. The Dual Contracts agreement of 1913 promoted massive extensions of both the BRT and IRT. In 1914 the BRT introduced its first steel cars. Longer and wider than those of the IRT, the difference in size made system integration impossible.

In November of 1885, the Staten Island Rail Road Company opened a 13-mile steam railway from Vanderbilt's Landing, Stapleton to Tottenville. The Baltimore & Ohio quickly bought the property, and went on to electrify it in 1925. Anticipating that a proposed tunnel to Brooklyn would be built, cars similar to the BMT's were bought for through service. In March, 1953, the Arlington and South Beach branches of the Staten Island Rapid Transit, as it came to be known, ceased operation. On July 1, 1971, the Staten Island Rapid Transit Operating Authority took over the line and received part of the city's R-44 car order.

In 1907 the New York Central Railroad began operating its first multiple-unit electric cars into Grand Central Terminal while construction of the Park Avenue tunnel was under way.

Just as Brooklyn had done in 1898, the western half of Queens County voted to join New York City in 1913 as a borough. Elevated lines formerly terminating at the old city line were extended into Queens. At the same time, some existing BMT els were rebuilt to accommodate heavier steel cars. Between 1913 and 1930 new subway lines of the BMT and IRT spread through Manhattan, the Bronx and Brooklyn and BMT trains began running over the Williamsburgh and Manhattan Bridges.

In 1927 a new subway network was planned by the city. Called the "Independent," since it was built independently of the existing companies, it used BMT specifications in hopes that the BMT would run it. However, the BMT went bankrupt as had the IRT earlier, and in 1940 the city wound up operating all the subway lines. The first section of IND to open was the Washington Heights line on September 10, 1932. In 1933 it was extended to Brooklyn, and when the Sixth Avenue subway opened December 14, 1940, the last major subway line had been completed. By 1941, all Manhattan els except Third Avenue and the portions of the Broadway line which still run today were gone.

The first electric buses were operated by the New York Department of Plant & Structures. Called "trollibuses," they began service in 1920 on Staten Island between Sea View Hospital and Bulls Head, and shortly thereafter to the Carteret Ferry in Travis. In 1927, both the trollibus and Midland Railway streetcar lines, also operated by the Department of Plant & Structures, ceased operating. Staten Island Edison refused to supply any more electric power because of an unpaid bill of $125,000.

In 1924, the Brooklyn Bus Company was formed to operate buses as feeders to Brooklyn streetcar lines and became a B&QT subsidiary in 1929. In 1930, the first electric buses in Brooklyn, called "trackless trolleys," began operating on the Cortelyou Road line. Six more lines would later be added, and it was envisioned that many bus routes would be converted to trackless trolley lines.

In 1936, the B&QT took delivery of the first PCC cars. The President's Conference Committee car was designed by a group of street railway executives to develop a modern streetcar that would lure back lost transit business. Third Avenue Railway modernized by building new cars of its own design in its own shops. But Mayor LaGuardia believed that buses were the modern way to go, and by World War II, only the Third Avenue Railway, B&QT, and Queensboro Bridge Railway operated streetcars.

Governmental intervention prevented further conversions to buses until the end of the war. The last streetcars ran in Manhattan in 1947, in the Bronx in 1948. Third Avenue Railway's rail service ended in Yonkers in 1952. While it had once been planned to equip more lines with PCC cars, Brooklyn's PCCs made their final runs in 1955. The trackless trolleys lasted only until 1960. Oddly, the city's last remaining streetcar line was the obscure and isolated Queensboro Bridge Railway which survived until 1957.

The unrebuilt sections of Brooklyn els disappeared one by one, the last being the Myrtle Avenue line from Broadway to Bridge & Jay Streets in 1969. With it, went the last wooden el cars. First-generation steel subway cars were replaced in the 1970s.

When the IND's Queens Boulevard subway line was planned, provision for a flying junction was made at the 63 Drive station to connect with the LIRR at White Pot Junction. Agreement could not be reached, and the subway did not reach the Rockaways until 1956 when the lower portion of the Rockaway line was linked to the IND at Liberty Avenue.

The year 1951 was a bad one for the LIRR. It had two major wrecks and its Jamaica Bay trestle was destroyed by fire. Placed in receivership, it wound up operated by the state. It is presently part of the Metropolitan Transit Authority, along with the New York City Transit Authority and Metro North which runs railroad commuter operations out of Grand Central.

The only subway extensions to be opened in recent years are the Archer Avenue line in Jamaica and the 63rd Street Tunnel line to Long Island City, which is to soon be connected to IND's Queens Boulevard line.

For years, a new surface rail line on Manhattan's 42nd Street has been talked about. Bids for construction of the right-of-way and cars are finally being sought. If completed, this will mark the first time in half a century that streetcars will have operated on 42nd Street, and the first time under wire.

The appearance of new transit proposals seems never ending. As an example, there have been proposals for rapid transit lines connecting all three major New York area airports. And as these ideas emerge, one thing is certain: the history of New York City transit is still being made.

Manhattan Memories

Manhattan's public transit is seen on these pages in three modes that were each evident within the span of a few years. Some were rapid, some not so rapid. The horsecar clopping westward along 23rd Street to one of the ferry services to New Jersey was a surviving vestige of the animal-powered transit that nearly choked the city as the Twentieth Century approached. An example of the vastly superior surface transit is New York Railways No. 452. Here the primitive piece of equipment is seen still threading its way along Broadway at Bowling Green in the mid-1930s. But in the world's mind, transit in New York City could only mean its fabulous subway system. A train of Interborough Rapid Transit's Lo-V cars working the Lexington Avenue line is seen making a service stop at 14th Street.

Author's collection

Richard Short collection

7

Copied from old postcard

With a distinctive carbody design said to cater to ladies wearing hobbleskirts, New York Railways actually set out to increase capacity with a second deck. A variation on a low-floor design, this innovative approach was applied to one experimental car, dubbed the "Broadway Battleship." Results were not favorable and the design was not repeated.

Walter Broschart, author's collection.

Rapid transit in downtown Manhattan is seen in two views taken a generation apart. Above ground, South Ferry was once served by the Third Avenue El. Heading uptown, a train of its cars snakes around the curves at Coenties Slip. Heading downtown, R-12 No. 5706 awaits departure at Bowling Green on the now-discontinued South Ferry shuttle.

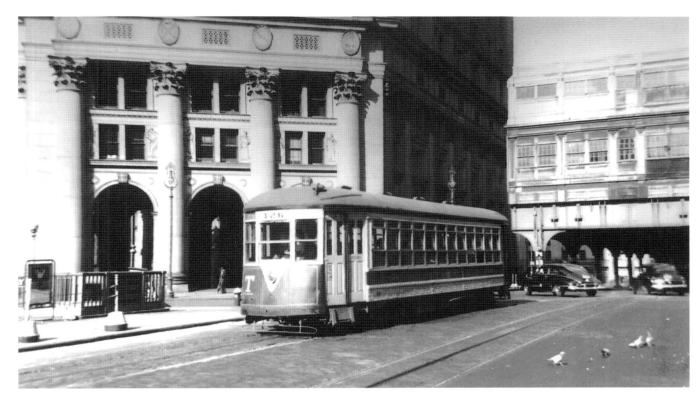

Walter Broschart, author's collection

A 1947 Pontiac with a body style called the "Streamliner" crosses in the wake of Third Avenue Railway's No. 126 at the Municipal Building. Having rolled out from under Third Avenue El's Park Row terminal, the streetcar nears the southern end of the T-Third & Amsterdam Aves. line at City Hall. Entrance to the Chambers Street station of the BMT's Centre Street subway is seen at the left.

Bill Myers collection

Lexington Avenue line's Worth Street station was closed for good about a month after this view was taken in 1960. It was replaced with a northward extension of the platforms of the Brooklyn Bridge station.

A wooden BMT el train leaves Park Row terminal headed for Brooklyn. At the time, both trolleys and els ran on the Brooklyn Bridge. Today, there is no public transportation on the bridge.

Vladimir Pincus collection

Fifth Avenue Coaches passed two of Manhattan's most celebrated landmarks, Pennsylvania Station on 7th Avenue and the arch at Washington Square in Greenwich Village. There was a noticable degree of regret that the double-deckers passed from the scene, but demolition of Penn Station inspired laws to preserve such fine structures.

Vladimir Pincus collection

On those occasional Manhattan days when the weather was perfect, there was little hope that upon climbing the spiral stairs one could find an empty seat on the open top. But how nice to re-member that No. 2019 once provided Manhat-tanites with just such an opportunity.

The Hudson & Manhattan Railroad, despite its regulators having guaranteed it a 6% return on investment, was starved of fare increases until it became a metropolitan embarassment. In 1964, this rail transit became an adjunct of the Port Authority which used the tubes to serve a gigantic World Trade Center complex which it set about to build. Rechristened the PATH, derived from Port Authority plus Trans-Hudson to form a most appropriate acronym, all signage was to be replaced but tilework such as this at the 14th Street and 6th Avenue IND station was still to be seen thirty years later. The platform view shows a southbound train from uptown arriving at 14th Street on May 16, 1964. Unlike today's travelers who pay a universal fare, its passengers to Newark had to buy an extra fare ticket and be buzzed through an iron gate bypass around the coin-operated turnstiles. The tickets were later taken up by "collectors" as the train left Jersey City's Journal Square station.

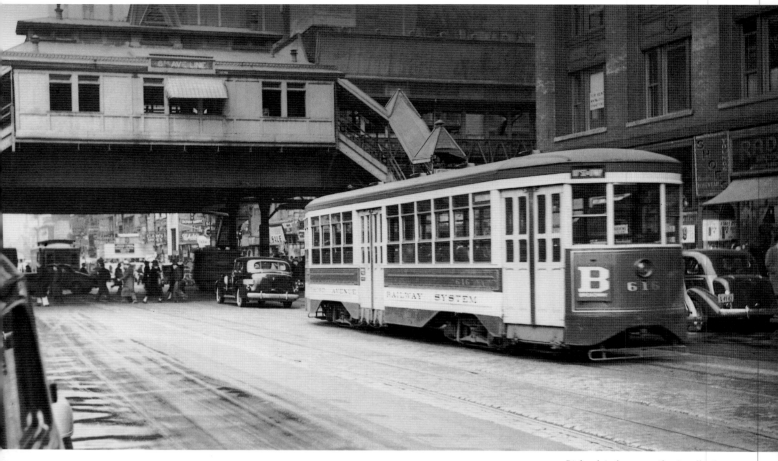

Richard Anderson, author's collection

Third Avenue Railway System, badly in need of new equipment in the mid-1930s, did not participate in the transit industry's collective effort to design a truly modern streetcar. Neither did it have the resources to buy the latest designs of the principal car builders. Necessity dictated that the company shops remanufacture a fleet of obsolete cars, salvaging what was useful and supplying new what was not. Aluminum-bodied, quiet, and comfortable, the new cars appeared in 1938. Guiding hand for this out-of-step with the industry approach was TARS president Huff and thus the cars were dubbed "Huffliners." No. 616 heads for Broadway as Route B crosses beneath the Sixth Avenue el's 42nd Street station. Despite public enthusiasm for the new cars, their service in Manhattan would be limited to a few years. City government hostility to street railway service was a continuing fact of life. Within a decade, most cars of this type were sold for use in the Brazilian city of São Paulo. As for the Sixth Avenue el, it was discontinued in 1938 preparatory to replacement by the IND subway which opened in 1940.

Walter Broschart, author's collection

Assigned to the 42nd Street Crosstown line, TARS lightweight 645 passes under the Third Avenue el. Already one block east of Grand Central Terminal, it continues crosstown. A painted legend on the rear door panel asks motorists to obey the 8 foot law.

Working westbound on the 42nd Street Crosstown line, TARS car 1050 moves past the Times Tower, a building which has made the Square famous for victory celebrations and ushering in new Januarys. The car is a convertible. Its floor-to-roof side panels were removed in summertime, much to the pleasure of sunny day riders.

Author's collection

George Votava, Melvin Rosenberg collection

New York Railways "breeze scooper" 4094 takes passengers downtown on Broadway at 17th Street in 1934. This early form of air conditioning ended in the mid-1930s due to the expense of keeping a second fleet of cars suitable only for warm weather.

Joe Guarino collection

About 1935, New York Railways semi-convertible car 546, assigned to the 34th Street Crosstown line, rested at the West 34th Street ferry. On a semi-convertible, only the window sections were removable for summer operation.

The lacy structure of the Queensboro Bridge looms large as TARS 627 waits at the First Avenue terminal of 59th Street's Crosstown line.

TARS "boxcar" enjoys the Columbus Circle statuary while working the X-59 ST. CROSSTOWN line in 1938.

Maximum traction trucks carry car 319 of the Eighth & Ninth Avenues Railway Company north on Central Park West. Passengers are seated on wooden benches arranged longitudinally.

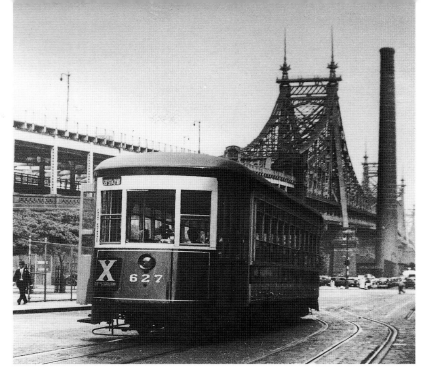

Richard Anderson, author's collection

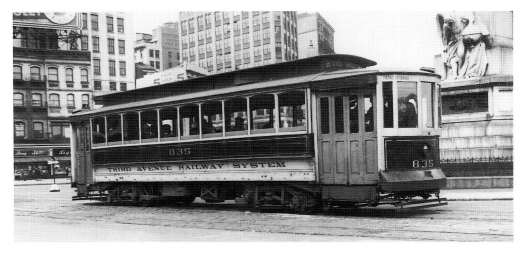

Joe Guarino collection

Mark D. Meyer, author's collection

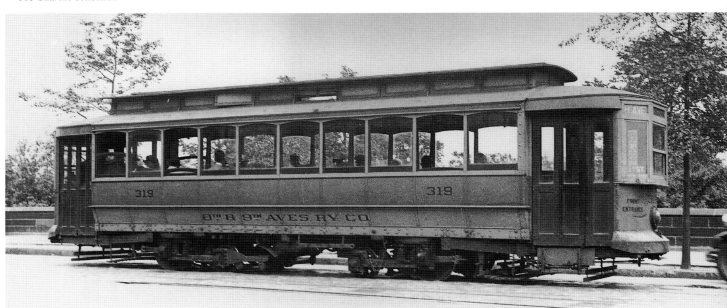

Both, Dennis Martlew, Rosenberg collection

Because the picturesque Third Avenue el was so long lasting, it ultimately became everyone's sentimental Manhattan favorite. These two street scenes capture the line as it was known to everyone, including those who never rode it. Above, a train accelerates northward out of 14th Steet Station while at right five cars rush north above the Bowery at Spring Street.

Walter Broschart, author's collection

The upper view of the Polo Grounds looks northwest toward Coogan's Bluff . Taken in 1948, it shows a two car shuttle from Sedgwick Avenue laying over on a portion of the old Ninth Avenue el. Below, taken in 1955, the camera aims northeast to show the swing bridge leading to the Sedgwick Avenue terminal of New York Central's Putnam Division. Having become useless after the Giants decamped to San Francisco in 1957 and "the Put" quit passenger operation in 1958, the shuttle was quickly abandoned.

Dennis Martlew, William Rosenberg collection

The operator of No. 605 waits for a young lady to make her mad dash to catch this northbound car. The point is 96th Street on the B-BROADWAY line.

TARS 399, eastbound on the T-THIRD & AMSTERDAM AVES line, has just passed under New York Central's station at Park Avenue and 125th Street.

Both, Walter Broschart, author's collection

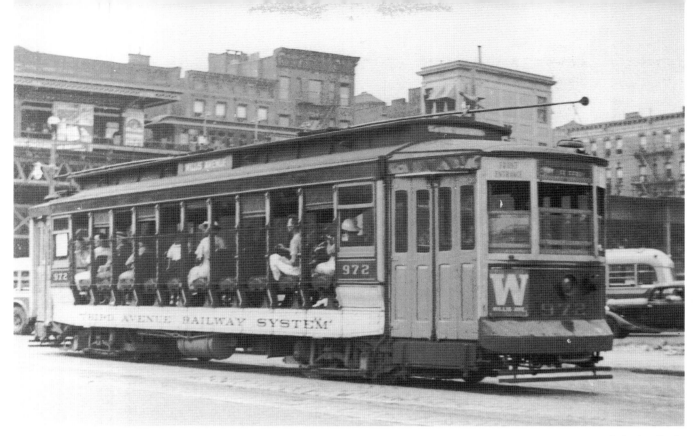

Author's collection

The balmy weather this July day in 1936 was ideal for a ride on TARS 972. Poles down, the car works the W-WILLIS AVE route toward Fort Lee Ferry. A 2nd Avenue el train is also here at its 125th Street Station.

By 1967, the Washington Square Inn owned Fifth Avenue Coach's 2124. Chartered by some fans that May 21, the vehicle paused at 145th Street and Lenox Avenue beside the last of the IRT subway entrance kiosks.

19

Memories of The Bronx

Author's collection

Third Avenue Railways car 292 steps gingerly onto the 138th Street bridge as it heads toward the Port Morris section of The Bronx. Only pre-World War II automobiles witnessed such crossings as streetcar service on the 138th Street Crosstown line was discontinued on July 10, 1940.

The Lo-V cars seen on the opposite page were in work service when this May 23, 1964 picture was taken. Only months earlier, they had provided service on the WOODLAWN-JEROME line. The scene was captured from the platform at Fordham Road station.

TARS 1238 emerges from the Grand Concourse underpass on the 163rd Street Crosstown line. The IND's subway entrance is just to the left of the car.

Although the Manhattan portion of the Third Avenue el quit running in 1956, the Bronx segment continued to operate. These R-12 cars were southbound in October, 1970 when this view was taken at 161st Street.

Walter Broschart, author's collection

TARS 1237, bought second-hand from San Antonio Public Service, working the X-163 ST. CROSSTOWN line, swings onto the 155th Street bridge in June of 1948.

Approaching the 155th Stret bridge, car 385 creeps ahead with traffic. Rail service on O-OGDEN AVE lasted only until October 25, 1947.

Author's collection

Walter Broschart, author's collection

Walter Broschart, author's collection

TARS 26 moves out of its layover point at 169th Street & Westchester Avenue. The car is headed for 181st Street and Broadway via its X-167 ST. CROSSTOWN line. The elevated structure in the background is the 6-PELHAM BAY el turning onto Westchester Avenue. The el will quickly bridge the tracks of both the New Haven and the New York, Westchester & Boston whose Westchester Avenue station is to the right of the bridge. Unseen just to the right is the Pelham Bay line's Whitlock Avenue station.

TARS 23 breezes into Fordham Square on the C-Bronx & VAN CORTLANDT PARKS line. This overhead view is from the Third Avenue el station.

From ground level at the Square, a Third Avenue el train pauses at the station as 970 loads westbound passengers on the C line.

Walter Broschart, author's collection

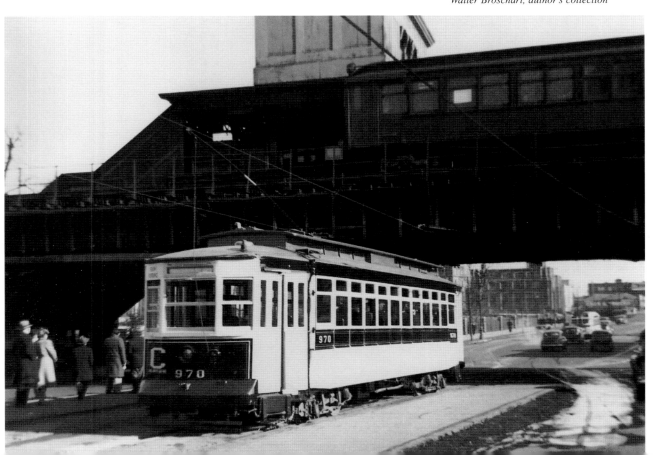

New Haven's service into Grand Central Terminal passes beneath the Third Avenue el just north of Fordham station. This inbound train is seen on April 21, 1963.

High above New York Central's Fordham station, a train of IRT's Worlds Fair-Steinway cars roars south toward its stop at Fordham Square station. The Third Avenue el's branch to the Botanic Gardens once diverged at a point in back of the train.

Unusual arch steelwork graces the Third Avenue el just south of Mosholu Parkway. This train of R-12's rumbled northward on November 8, 1969.

The scene is Gun Hill Road station in April of 1963. The upper level train with R-29 No. 8972 on the rear is on the White Plains Road line. The lower level belongs to the Third Avenue el. Worlds Fair 5677, still lettered for the IRT, awaits departure.

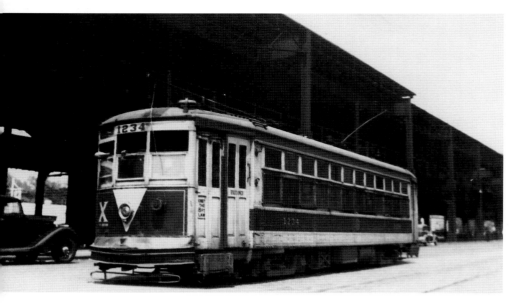

Below Gun Hill Road station, sequential car number 1234 made a fan trip photo stop on White Plains Road.

Walter Broschart, author's collection

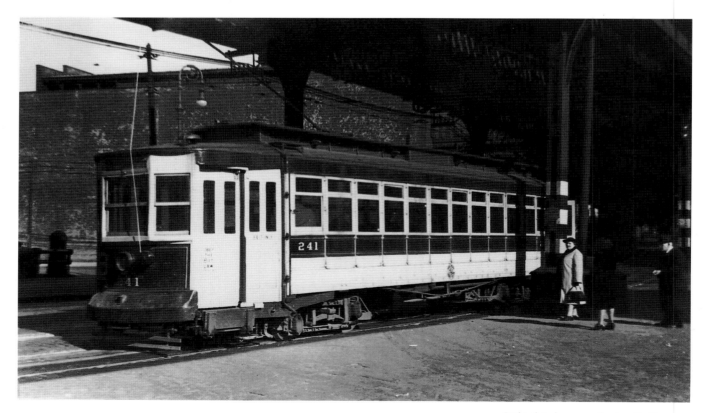

Richard Anderson, author's collection

Under the White Plains Road el, TARS 241 completes a service stop on the B-BOSTON ROAD line.

Assigned to the A-WESTCHESTER AVE line, TARS 239 changes ends under the IRT Pelham line el at Westchester and Tremont Avenues.

Arnold Joseph

Joe Guarino collection

With its side panels removed for summer operation, TARS 236 waits invitingly at the Pelham Bay el line terminal for passengers wishing to ride the P-PELHAM BAY line.

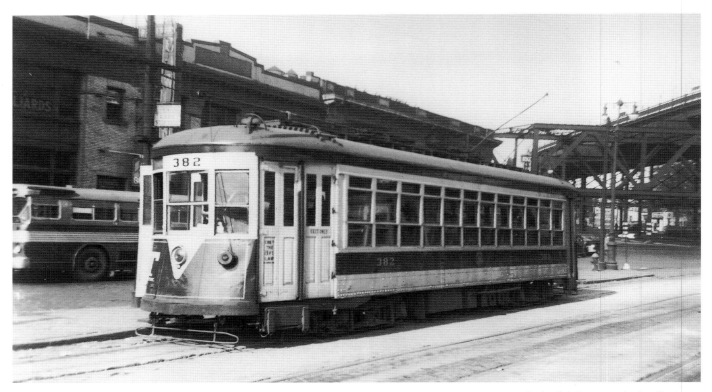

Richard Anderson, author's collection

Looking west at West Farms Square, TARS 382 loads passengers on the T-TREMONT line. So too does the Twin Coach bus on North Shore Bus Company's Q-44 BRONX-JAMAICA route.

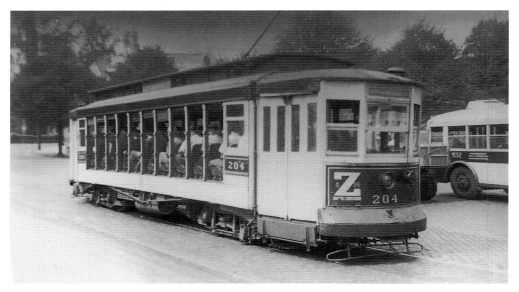

Walter Broschart, author's collection

Convertible 284 fitted for summertime operation handles a full passenger load on the Z-180 ST. CROSSTOWN line. Traffic at Fordham Road includes Surface Transit's bus 932, but it runs empty this hot day.

Walter Broschart, author's collection

Wooden cars from IRT's Second Avenue El were resurrected for the Dyre Avenue Shuttle where they finished out their days. The shuttle, opened in 1941, used the right-of-way of the New York, Westchester, & Boston RR which had been abandoned three years earlier. Relic 1585 heads a southbound train at Morris Park.

Author's collection

In a wartime view taken in July of 1943, TARS 651 stops on Morris Park Avenue at the East 180th Street station.

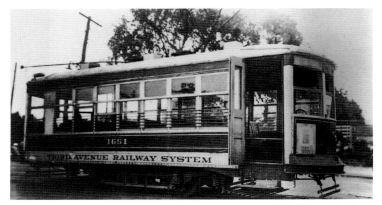

Starting in 1917, TARS Westchester County Route D extended to Conner & Givan Avenues, the site of a boat basin on the now-filled-in Hutchinson River. The capacity of Birney 1651 was more than ample for this feeder to NYW&B's Dyre Avenue station. In 1922, the line was cut back to Dyre Avenue.

S. B. Olsen collection

Walter Broschart, author's collection

Passengers impatiently await the changing of ends on TARS 1143. The car will soon enough leave the Route V-WILLIAMSBRIDGE terminus at Tremont and Third Avenues and find its way back out White Plains Road to the Gun Hill Road terminus.

Walter Broschart, author's collection

This is Broadway and 242nd Street where The Bronx streetcars met the Yonkers streetcars. A uniformed starter kept operations orderly if delays and traffic conditions disrupted the usual order of things.

Memories Grow in Brooklyn

Perhaps one of the inspirations for Evans and Shields when they composed *In the Good Old Summertime* was the joy of riding an open car. That was in 1902, and two decades later, Brooklyn & Queens No. 491 was still rolling along Church Avenue en route to Utica Avenue.

John H. Riley collection

The advertising boards on the dash of BRT summer car 743 proclaim Luna Park, one of Coney Island's three great amusement parks, is a "world of fun." First Dreamland, then Luna Park were destroyed by fire. Steeplechase, the oldest, survived only to go out of business quietly.

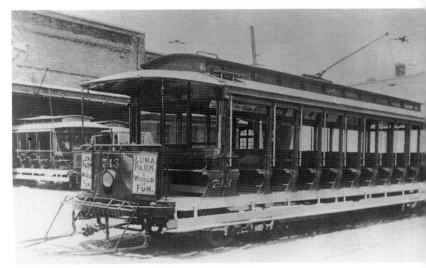

Richard Anderson, author's collection

Opposite, the Brooklyn of November 5, 1954 was captured on film just at at the point where film star Alan Ladd was dealing—not with summertime—but with *Hell Below Zero*. PCC 1013 is seen passing the Beverly theater as it works latter-day Route 35-CHURCH.

Both, Walter Broschart, author's collection

City Hall in Manhattan provides a back-drop for the B&QT PCC cars that linked the borough of Manhattan with the borough of Brooklyn. No. 1027 sits on one of the multiple loop tracks forming the Park Row terminal at the foot of the Brooklyn Bridge.

Coming into Park Row off Brooklyn's Route 67-SEVENTH AVENUE, No. 1089 drops downgrade out of the truss work and into the sunshine.

William Rosenberg collection

Rails and wires filled downtown Brooklyn in yesteryear. An Oldsmobile crowds between PCC 1097 in service on the 67-SEVENTH AVE line and trackless 3091 operating on the 45-ST. JOHNS. The location is the Long Island Railroad terminal at Flatbush & Atlantic Avenues with the post office building in the background.

The building in the background of B&QT 6062 working the PUTNAM line is Borough Hall.

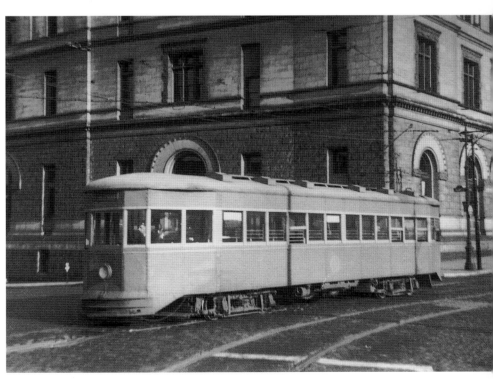

Walter Broschart, author's collection

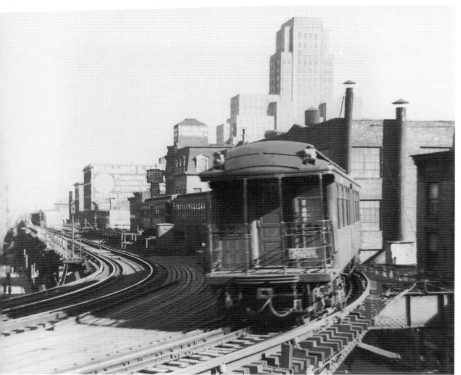

BMT Q-types were assigned to the Myrtle line in this August 7, 1960. This train cruises into Navy Street to make one of its regular ports of call.

A decade earlier, open platform wooden cars operated out of Sands Street. This train squealed around the turn west of Bridge & Jay Streets station onto the structure over Myrtle Avenue itself.

Walter Broschart, author's collection

Joe Guarino collection

A 1940 view looking south from the Fulton Street el down Flatbush Avenue reveals the 5th Avenue elevated with a trolley turning beneath it.

The BMT's BU convertibles are seen passing on the Lexington Avenue line.

Walter Broschart, author's collection

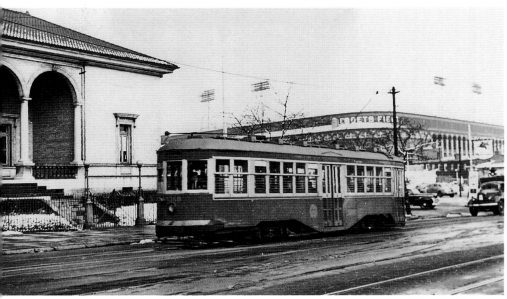

Bill Myers collection

Nationwide, Brooklyn's two most symbolic structures were its bridge and its ball park. B&QT 8360 rambles along Empire Boulevard with traces of snow to be seen. Can the Dodgers season be far behind?

On April 23, 1960, NYCTA 3095 on Route 47-TOMPKINS passes the intersection of Empire Boulevard and McKeever Place. The Dodgers, like the streetcar tracks, are gone, and even the ball park's days were numbered.

B&QT sweeper 9842 battles snowflakes on Court Street at Livingston Street. The sweepers were quite effective as streetcar routes were always the first arteries to be cleared.

Art Ward, author's collection

A B&QT TOMPKINS AVE line trolley heads for the Delancey Street subway terminal in Manhattan. Within view of the Williamsburgh Savings Bank, the car climbs the approach to the Driggs Avenue station in the shadow of Brooklyn's Broadway elevated line as it too makes the bridge crossing.

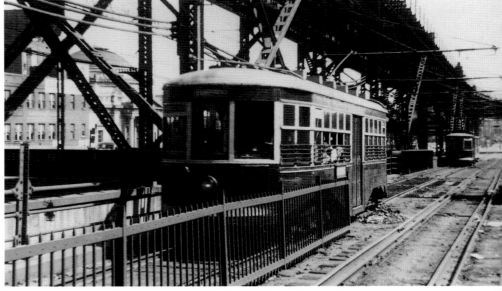

Both, Walter Broschart, author's collection

B&QT's GRAND ST line served by car 8364 heads for Junction Avenue. It passes under the Williamsburgh Bridge heading north on Driggs Avenue. The bank building, seen between the girders of the bridge, helps orient the viewer.

Trolley coach 3085 on the 47-TOMPKINS line passes under the Broadway Brooklyn el at Williamsburgh Bridge Plaza as a brand new first generation GM "fishbowl" bus begins its career on a wintery March day in 1960.

41

There's no stop on the Myrtle Avenue el where it crosses Wilson Avenue. No. 8420 pushes forward toward Cooper Avenue and the run down Rockaway Avenue through Brownsville to Canarsie Depot.

Judging from the sharp angle with which the front wheels point inward on Sabrett's truck, the hot dogs are stranded. Perhaps that's the driver standing near No. 8431 objecting to having the predicament recorded on film. Actually, the cameraman's focus is on the streetcar and the Broadway el's Marcy Avenue station here in the heart of Williamsburgh.

Both, William Rosenberg collection

On its way to Williamsburgh, B&QT 8329 meets another Wilson Avenue car as it crosses Broadway on the transition from Rockaway Avenue to Cooper Avenue.

No. 8403 plods onward at Union & Johnson Avenues in the Williamsburgh section as it nears the line's terminus.

Despite the blank destination signs, B&QT 8085 is assigned to a regular route, the short Holy Cross Cemetery shuttle . This view of changing ends at the ivy-covered gates was taken shortly before World War II, with rail service not ending until New Years Day, 1951.

Walter Broschart, author's collection

Bill Myers collection

Whereas production line streamliners were built by St. Louis Car Co. and by Pullman-Standard, Clark Equipment did make the initial effort and built one car to the specifications of the Presidents Conference Committee. Its body design was unlike the production models and that uniqueness has saved it for museum preservation. The one of a kind sits at Bristol Street loop of the 35-CHURCH line.

Another modern design is displayed by NYCTA 3095 on Route 47-TOMPKINS as it leaves behind the Myrtle Avenue el.

Author's collection

In this pre-war scene, the older equipment to serve Brooklyn is typified by No. 2535 growling along on the Bushwick line under the el at Myrtle & Wyckoff Avenues.

The Fulton Street el station at Ralph Avenue looked quite spruce in 1940. No. 8446 is seen executing its assignment to the RALPH ROCKAWAY line.

William Rosenberg collection

Art Ward

B&QT 6032 on the MYRTLE COURT line rolls along Court Street at Sackett Street. There are elements of this neighborhood scene that haven't changed much since the 19th century.

Walter Broschart, author's collection

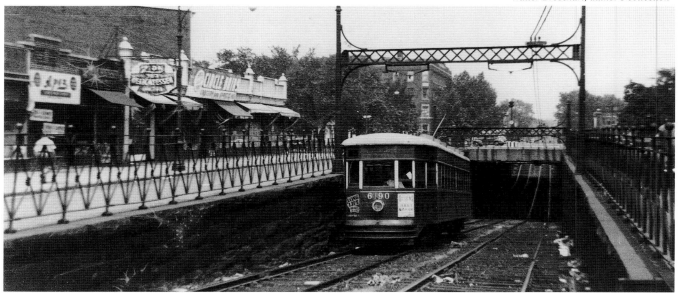

William Rosenberg collection

The CHURCH AVE line ducked under Ocean Parkway on a short stretch of private right-of-way. B&QT 6190 hums uphill through the litter.

In another selected view of a 6000-series car, 6069 poses quietly on a private right-of-way siding.

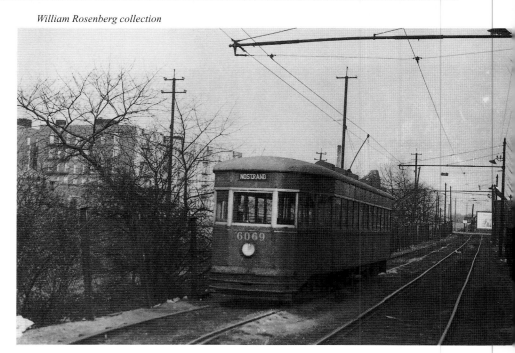

Bill Myers collection

PCC 1041 is seen passing under the IND's massive structure over the Gowanus Canal. During construction of the crossing in 1931, streetcar operations were reduced to a shuttle service on Smith Street. The car wears its original color scheme of gray with a red stripe.

PCC 1010, the only one with a GM bus roof vent, is also seen operating on Route 68-SMITH-CONEY ISLAND. A Kaiser sedan follows the car around the circle at Bartel-Pritchard Square.

Walter Broschart, author's colledction

Richard Anderson, author's collection

PCC 1013 passes the Sea Breeze Hotel on Sea Breeze Avenue as it serves Route 63-CONEY ISLAND, a route not established until the summer of 1946.

B&QT 5099, a former center entrance car converted to one-man operation, makes a stop in Coney Island on Surf Avenue on the SEA GATE line at West 8th Street. The New York Aquarium now occupies the land across the street from the Famous Bar.

Author's collection

Walter Broschart, author's collection

B&QT 4703 on the ROCKAWAY PARKWAY line loads passengers at the terminal of BMT's 14 ST-CANARSIE line. Cut back from Canarsie shore, the line was ended at this point in 1928 on the occasion of the subway line from Manhattan being connected to the Canarsie el.

The NORTONS POINT line was an extension of a BMT rapid transit line. B&QT 5082 steals through the back yards of Coney Island.

Art Ward, author's collection

At 9th Avenue, the Culver line branched from the BMT's West End line, surfaced and in less than a mile reached the Ditmas Avenue station en route to Coney Island. In 1941, construction started on an extension to the Independent subway from its Church Avenue station to the BMT's elevated station at Ditmas Avenue. Interrupted by the war, the connection was not completed until 1954 when Coney Island service ran via the IND and the link between 9th Avenue and Ditmas Avenue became a shuttle service. Serving little purpose, the Culver shuttle was finally abandoned in 1974.

Odds and ends of equipment were assigned to the Culver shuttle. One such type were Lo-V cars from the IRT which were modified with "skirts" to allow these narrow cars to meet up with platforms built to accommodate the wide cars of the BMT. On August 7, 1960, some Lo-Vs wait at the now-unused lower level station at 9th Avenue.

An interior view was taken as the car waited out its layover time at Ditmas Avenue.

Staten Island Rapid Transit cars were built to conform to BMT specifications in anticipation of a subway tunnel between Brooklyn and Richmond Boroughs. When the cars were replaced on Staten Island, they were brought over for further use in Brooklyn. A short train of them is seen at Ditmas Avenue on October 12, 1958.

A train of C type cars, 3-car articulated trains made from open platform wooden cars, heads toward the Rockaway Avenue terminal of the the truncated Fulton Street el. A Twin Coach bus rolls westbound on Fulton Street.

The passing of a friend known as Myrtle, or simply the Myrt, came in the pleasant weather of October 5, 1969. The memorable trains to serve this Bridge & Jay Streets terminal were making their last runs.

After the Manhattan Bridge track was severed from the Centre Street subway, Coney Island yard was reached via the Montague Street tunnel. The restricted height required lowering the roofline as seen on the Q-type train at the left compared to the train at the right. This Myrtle Avenue el scene is at Broadway.

The "Million dollar train," as these unique R-11 cars were termed, makes a rare visit to the East 105th Street grade crossing in Canarsie on the Fourth of July, 1966. This grade crossing on the 14 ST-CANARSIE line was the last on the system. Ultimately, the street was eliminated when industrial development altered the area.

On August 9, 1969, the R-42s were the city's newest rail equipment and the oldest cars were the 66-year old Q types. In a scene that would be ended in two months, they are found juxtaposed at Broadway and Myrtle.

Route 62-GRAHAM passengers on trackless 3067 witness the brisk pace of the banana business at Debvoise Street. It was March 12, 1960, and in four months this form of transport would vanish from the streets of New York City.

An interior view of trolley coach 3045 in action.

Queens Memories

Until abandoned in 1941, IRT's 2nd Avenue el reached Queensboro Plaza via the Queensboro Bridge. This light traffic view was taken in 1937.

Mark Douglas collection

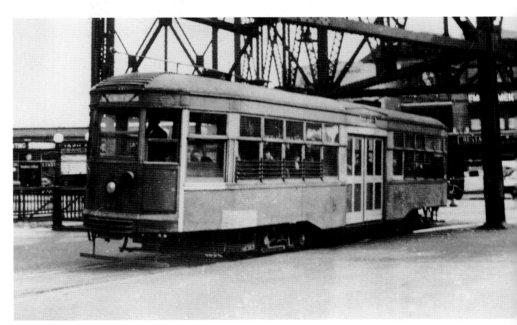

Manhattan & Queens Railway built streetcar tracks over the Queensboro Bridge and operated a surface car service between the two boroughs. M&Q car 112 passes the entrance to the IND subway Queens Plaza station beneath the junction of the Flushing and Astoria elevated lines on Queens Boulevard and Jackson Avenue.

Bill Myers collection

The network of trackless trolley routes as it survived in 1960 throughout Brooklyn and Queens ended in one fell swoop on July 24 of that year. Coach 3074 was on a fan trip when it was photographed crossing the Long Island Rail Road on Flushing Avenue in Maspeth that final day.

Walter Broschart, author's collection

Walter Broschart, author's collection

Queensboro Bridge Railway's Osgood-Bradley Master Unit 607 came from the New Bedford, Massachusetts streetcar system after it abandoned rail service. The car moves through the lacy shadows at Queensboro Plaza.

With the simple destination sign of NEW YORK, the bridge line's 536 rests on the curved rail at the end of the line at Queensboro Plaza.

On May 6, 1962, the platforms on the north side of Queensboro Plaza station were being dismantled as a train of R-30 cars on the QB line pauses on its way to Astoria. Some of the no longer used structure still remains as it is needed to support the rest of the complex.

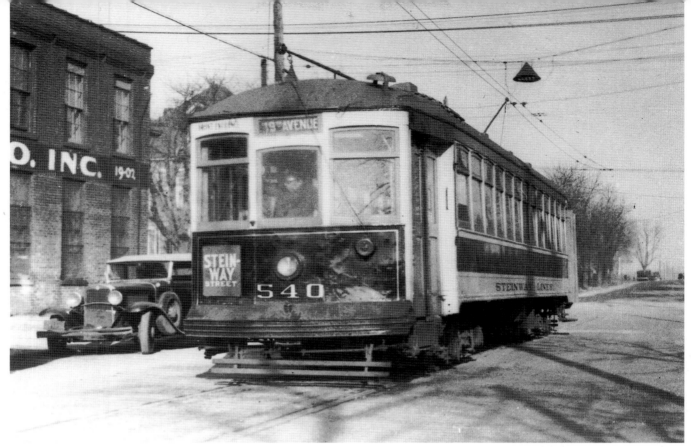

Walter Broschart, author's collection

Steinway Lines 540 waits at the northern end of the STEINWAY STREET line at 19th Avenue in 1936.

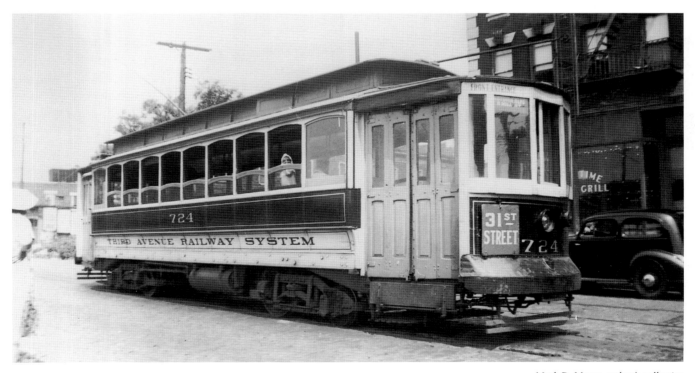

Mark D. Meyer, author's collection

Deck roof car 724 was on loan to Steinway Lines by its parent company, Third Avenue Railway. The child in the car waves goodbye to Mommy on Astoria Boulevard at Mill Street on July 13, 1938.

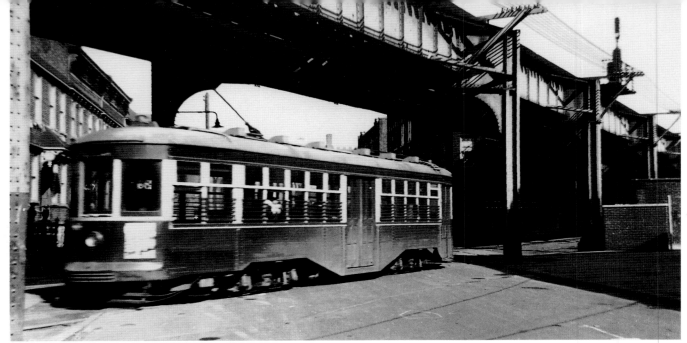

Walter Broschart, author's collection

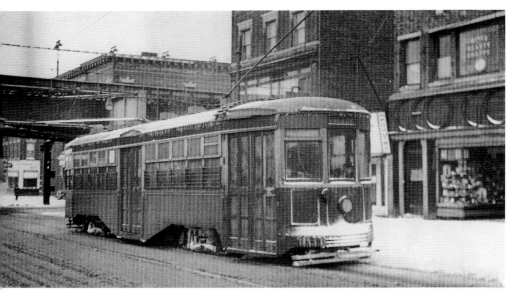

A FLUSHING RIDGEWOOD car heads east on its private right-of-way underneath the Myrtle Avenue el. No. 8495 is seen negotiating the crossing at Madison Street.

At Fresh Pond Road, snow-decorated 8435 is about to enter the private right-of-way.

Richard Short collection

The first buses to replace the **FLUSHING RIDGEWOOD** trolleys in July of 1949 were Twin Coaches like 1472. The line was renamed 58-CORONA and its route involved zigzagging on narrow streets running diagonally to the old trolley right of way. The scene is at the Fresh Pond Road el

Mark D. Meyer, author's collection

B&QT sweeper on the FLUSHING RIDGEWOOD line is barely challenged by the flakes of a Washington's Birthday snowfall in 1948. The slight upgrade is the 61st Street hill in Maspeth.

This is the Maspeth depot at Grand Avenue and Brown Place as seen in its last days of operation. Today, the Long Island Expressway cuts through this site.

Walter Broschart, author's collection

The bright sunshine of July 5, 1963 and the openness of the platforms at 36th Avenue Astoria made for a fine portraiture of BMT types B and D in service on the West End line.

Dennis Martlew, William Rosenberg collection

The Myrtle Avenue el extended far from its terminal in the heart of Brooklyn into Queens County. There, it operated at ground level past Lutheran Yard at Fresh Pond Road and on to its terminal at Metropolitan Avenue. Having made the run, convertible 1382 rests at the platform awaiting its return trip.

Remodeled IND R-7a car 1575, the prototype for the R-10 series, waits at the head end of a QJ train at the 168th Street station in Jamaica. The date is March 11, 1972. The Valencia theatre has since become a church. 1575 is now part of the New York Transit Museum collection.

The lineup at Fresh Pond yard on March 14, 1959 featured the youngest to the oldest equipment at the time. From left to right: Q type of 1903, Multi-section articulated of 1934, B type of 1914-1923 period, and an R-16 of 1954-1955.

A train of R-38 cars pauses at the Playland station on May 20, 1970 on what had been an LIRR line. The roller coaster of the station's namesake "Rockaways Playland," an amusement park, can be seen at right. A housing development now fills the site.

There's a lot of bygone elements in this July 14, 1962 photo taken at 131st Street & Jamaica Avenue. The elevated structure itself has been removed. The line was cut back back to the other side of the LIRR main line and connected to the Archer Avenue subway. The R-16 cars were retired. The Westbridge LIRR station whose brick structure entrance is seen was discontinued in 1928. And finally, the beloved Bungalow Bars are among the missing.

Walter Broschart collection

New York & Queens County Transit operated a significant streetcar network comprised of five lines in Queens. One of these was a north-south route between College Point and Jamaica. Car 22 sits at College Point Ferry shortly before all lines were abandoned in 1937.

Willaim Rosenberg collection

Jamaica Central Railways operated two lines out of Jamaica, one to Far Rockaway, the other to Belmont Park. Abandonment came in 1933. Car 603 shows off its maximum traction trucks outside the car barn.

Walter Broschart, author's collection

B&QT 8381 on the JAMAICA line waits on Jamaica Avenue at Crescent Street for the bus running on the 13-CRESCENT ST line to pull away from the curb. The entrance to the Cypress Hills station of the Broadway-Jamaica el lies across the street. Until the el was extended to Jamaica in 1916, the station was at a right angle to Jamaica Avenue where the line terminated.

Richard Anderson, author's collection

B&QT 5063 clatters over the crossing with the Long Island Rail Road's Old Montauk branch. The car is heading west on the FLUSHING AVE line. The grade crossing has since been eliminated by depressing Flushing Avenue beneath the tracks.

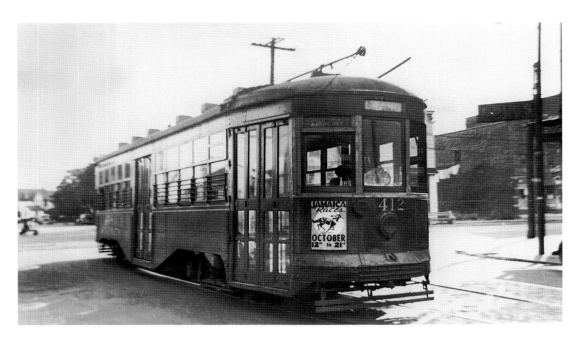

B&QT 8412 on the GRAND line turns onto Junction Boulevard from Corona Avenue. The car heads for North Beach Airport, built on the site of the North Beach Amusement Park. The advertising board announces horse races at the now-closed Jamaica Race Track.

Both, Walter Boschart, author's collection

Southbound on the GRAND line's route down Junction Boulevard, car 8321 passes under the Long Island Rail Road's Port Washington line at an interesting moment.

Walter Broschart, author's collection

Before being shipped to Branford Electric Railway's museum in Connecticut, B&QT's convertible 4573 was taken for a fan trip in 1948. At the Flushing end of the FLUSHING RIDGEWOOD line, the chartered car rolled past the Prospect Theatre on Main Street. Not only are all the streetcars long gone from downtown Flushing, so are all the movie theatres.

Mark D. Meyer, author's collection

The fan trip visited La Guardia airport, as the old North Beach Airport had been renamed. At the extreme right, there's a boy who has gotten off his bicycle to watch activities, proceedings he has found to be more fascinating than watching airplanes take off and land.

A train of brand-new blue-and-white R-36 cars on the Worlds Fair Super Express passes a local at Rawson Street on May 9, 1964.

The Transit Authority offered all states the opportunity to sponsor a Worlds Fair car. Five states—Kansas, Missouri, Massachusetts, Vermont, and as seen here, Rhode Island—accepted the offer.

William Rosenberg collection

The other great people mover to serve the Worlds Fair was the Long Island Rail Road. Here a bi-level is spotted on one of the platform tracks at the fair grounds.

A generous snowfall on February 10, 1969 delayed NYCTA 670 as it slugged it out on 67th Avenue near 60th Place in Ridgewood. Route 20 is the DECATUR route with this run hoping to reach Ashford Street.

Walter Broschart, author's collection

In 1912, the BMT planned to extend its Fulton Street el from Grant Avenue to Jamaica, but Lefferts Boulevard was as far as it got. Here the Lefferts Boulevard platform is shared by a train of C type wooden articulated cars on the right with a train of lightweight Multi-section 5-car articulateds. The Multis are working the 14th Street-Fulton line, a rush-hour only service that ended in 1956 when connection with the 14th Street-Canarsie line was changed to a connection with the IND at Hudson Street.

The Hollis station is still in service but the attractive old 19th-century Victorian station was destroyed by fire just a few months after this photo was taken on September 4, 1967.

Walter Broschart, author's collection

Bellaire station is one of the stations in New York City that was closed due to competition from nearby transit lines.

Staten Island Memories

In an early experiment, the city's Department of Plant & Structures tried the idea of operating a bus propelled by electricity from overhead wires. A second wire was needed for the return circuit since the rails that streetcars used for that purpose weren't available. The solid rubber tires were harsh riding not only for the passengers but also the equipment. Results, given the technology at hand, were unacceptable and operations were not long-lived. This scene is at the Castleton Corners loop.

Joe Guarino collection

The rail operation of the city's department was the Staten Island Midland Railway. Car 304 signed MIDLAND is stopped in the rain at Hamilton Street.

On the opposite page with gates down, the crossing at New Dorp is protected for a westbound local. It is August 25, 1963 and Mitchell's stylish Sunoco station is ready for customers who would rather drive their own car than ride the Staten Island Rapid Transit's public conveyance.

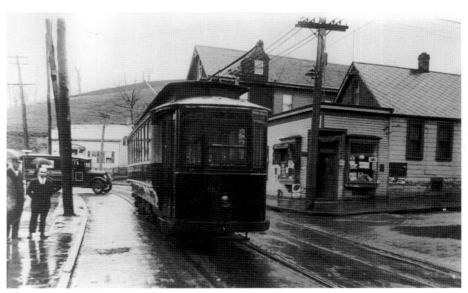

Joe Guarino collection

All, Joe Guarino collection

The Staten Island Midland Railway was operated by the New York Department of Plant & Structures. At top, car 321 operates side-of-the-road down Richmond Turnpike at Clove Road. The turnpike was to become Victory Boulevard.

Inbound car 312 nearly grazes a front yard fence as it squeezes along the road en route to "N. Y. FERRY."

Birney safety car 137 moves away from the camera and Port Richmond toward St. George. There were two routes between St. George and Port Richmond, one via Richmond Terrace past Sailors Snug Harbor and the other at a higher elevation via Castleton Avenue.

Both, Joe Guarino collection

Motorbus service was well established when this scene of the St. George ferry terminal plaza was taken on April 15, 1920. Streetcars 309 and 312 head up a four car array waiting for the next boat load of passengers. Operations were dispatched from a turret mounted on the corner of the company offices.

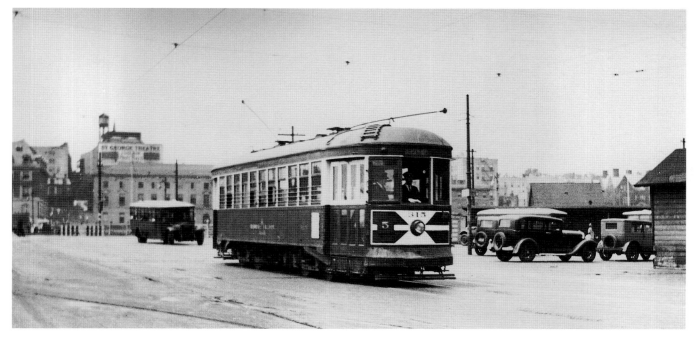

On July 20, 1933, Richmond Railways 315 and a primitive bus moved across the plaza of the ferry terminal. The car is operating on Route 5, JERSEY ST, a fairly short local route within the St. George and New Brighton areas.

Bound for Tottenville, this train makes a stop at Clifton, formerly the junction point for the South Beach branch. The brick tower lasted into the late 1980s before being demolished.

A South Beach train sits at the end of the line at Wentworth Avenue.

Walter Broschart, author's collection

A westbound train for Tottenville arrives at the Pleasant Plains station in October, 1964 when the venerable old wooden station was still in fairly good condition. It later suffered from vandalism and was finally destroyed by fire.

The flight of the tail fins on a 1958 Plymouth hardtop is momentarily delayed by the low-flying Staten Island Rapid Transit. No. 386 was lead car on this eastbound train at Guyon Avenue, Oakwood Heights on September 3, 1962.

In 1927, a grade crossing separation project was begun at Oakwood Heights and Bay Terrace. Temporary shoo-fly tracks and stations were built and the old line removed before the Great Depression struck. The project was revived in the mid-1960s. When completed, attention was turned to the remaining grade crossings. Here at Peter Avenue on May 14, 1966, a westbound train leaves the temporary track through New Dorp and Grant City and heads for the new Oakwood Heights station.

A single car uses the westbound temporary bypass track at Grant City. The new station construction was well along on November 11, 1967. Retaining walls for the depressed level trackage can be seen at left.

On its way to Tottenville, a train leaves the westbound platform of the temporary Jefferson Avenue station on April 29, 1967. To increase visibilty, car ends received a coat of light gray paint.

In their latter years, SIRT cars wore a dark blue paint job. This eastbound train displays that treatment at Grant City's temporary station on May 14, 1966.

A train for Tottenville eases to a stop at the bucolic Princess Bay station on August 25, 1963. Being the middle of a hot summer Sunday, two cars were more than adequate for the run.

In the late 1960s, the SIRT borrowed some Long Island Rail Road MP-85 MU cars to supplement its roster. The Long Island was in receipt of its M-1s while Staten Island was awaiting delivery of some R-44s. The move worked well as the Long Island cars rode quite comfortably on SIRT's track. On August 30, 1972, two MP-85s were chartered for an NRHS fantrip and are seen here on the gentle curve at Princess Bay.

On a June day in 1960, SIRT 4-wheel snow sweeper X-600 dozes at the St. George terminal, its single pair of third rail shoes just beyond the end of the third rail. Although it was not self-propelled, this piece of equipment was perfect for cleaning up the grade crossings.

The 6000-series Mack buses began their service life in Brooklyn and finished out their days on Staten Island. Here, 6002 on the R-112 line heads south on New Dorp Lane on November 11, 1967.

Demolition and Preservation

Dennis Masrtlew, William Rosenberg collection

Not sure where to put Third Avenue el cars while they waited for the scrapper, the New York City Transit Authority found a place on abandoned New York, Westchester & Boston right-of-way. Some fellows with rocks and stones also found them.

[OPPOSITE PAGE:]

Gruesome as it may seem, this scrap yard scene at Coney Island represents millions of miles of transit service that have been provided to the traveling public. While these particular vehicles are physically exhausted and obsolete in technology, the transit infrastructure of the city has been updated and advanced. The date is November 9, 1963, a time when the 20-year economic life of model TDH buses from General Motors expired concurrently with the 43-year life of the BMT's subway cars.

Bill Volkmer, author's collection

In a during-the-war and after-2nd Avenue el-abandonment time frame, a number of the ancient wooden cars were shipped to Oakland. California to carry shipyard workers. A lucky few found themselves saved for the operating museum at Rio Vista.

Richard Anderson, author's collection

In an after-the-war and after-TARS-abandonment time frame, some of the modern cars found employment outside the United States. Renumbered 1771, this car served the residents of São Paulo, Brazil.

This ex-TARS streetcar had a second career in Vienna, Austria where it was renumbered 4239. After being retired a second time, it had a glorious return home to the United States. After display in Central Park on May 27, 1967, it went on to a third career at the trolley museum at Branford, Connecticut.

Several B&QT PCC car bodies, painted in differing pastel colors, were used as dormitories at the Brooklyn Day Camp at the Hammels in Rockaway, Queens.

Yes, it's a IND subway car with a trolley pole. And the Hudson & Manhattan car behind it has one too. While not authentic, it's the difference between a static display and the opportunity to operate the car over the line at Branford.

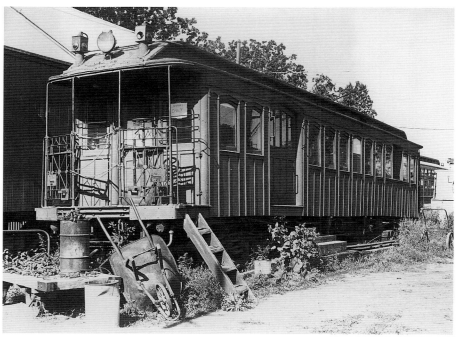

IRT pay car G is seen on the museum property at Branford.

Bill Volkmer, author's collection

B&QT 8111 typifies the amount of work needed to restore a streetcar and the care which is applied in such a project. The front of the car has been restored and primed and the roof over the front platform has been renewed. The volunteer effort is on-going and enjoys public support.

Unique Clark-built PCC 1000 was stored for the New York Trolley Museum in St. George, Staten Island in 1962. Currently destined for an operating museum in Kingston, New York, the car has been restored in the Coney Island shop.

Built in anticipation of a 2nd Avenue subway in Brooklyn, a short stub end of the IND subway system extends into a station at Court Street . Valueless as part of a transportation network, the spur was operated as the HH-COURT ST. SHUTTLE until near-zero patronage caused service to be discontinued. Then used for storage, movie-making, and publicity photos, this short section of subway's value as a museum became recognized and it exhibitions became reality. Visitors enter down a regular subway station stairway at Schermerhorn Street & Boerum Place as seen at top left. The mezzanine level has rare maps, displays of signals and turnstiles, a gift shop, and mockups of equipment facades such as the B&QT streetcar seen top right. At platform level, vistors are treated to a large scale model of an R-10 subway car, bottom left, and a variety of bygone subway system equipment, some of which are seen at bottom right.

[INSIDE BACK COVER:]
B&QT's historic PCC 1001 has been beautifully restored at Branford. In this 1965 photo, it poses on trackage in the meadowlands of shoreline Connecticut.